MATH IN OUR WORLD

GRAPHING
FAVORITE THINGS

By Jennifer Marrewa
Photographs by Patrick Espinosa

Reading consultant: Susan Nations, M.Ed.,
author/literacy coach/consultant in literacy development
Math consultant: Rhea Stewart, M.A., mathematics content specialist

WEEKLY READER®
PUBLISHING

Please visit our web site at **www.garethstevens.com**
For a free color catalog describing our list of high-quality books,
call 1-800-542-2595 (USA) or 1-800-387-3178 (Canada). Our fax: 1-877-542-2596

Library of Congress Cataloging-in-Publication Data

Marrewa, Jennifer.
     Graphing favorite things / Jennifer Marrewa.
          p. cm. — (Math in our world. Level 2)
        ISBN-13: 978-0-8368-9008-2 (lib. bdg.)
        ISBN-10: 0-8368-9008-6 (lib. bdg.)
        ISBN-13: 978-0-8368-9017-4 (softcover)
        ISBN-10: 0-8368-9017-5 (softcover)
        1. Mathematics—Graphic methods—Juvenile literature. 2. Mathematics—
Charts, diagrams, etc.—Juvenile literature. I. Title.
QA40.5.M377   2008
001.4'226—dc22   2007033376

This edition first published in 2008 by
Weekly Reader® Books
An Imprint of Gareth Stevens Publishing
1 Reader's Digest Road
Pleasantville, NY 10570-7000 USA

Senior Editor: Brian Fitzgerald
Creative Director: Lisa Donovan
Graphic Designer: Alexandria Davis

Printed in the United States

1 2 3 4 5 6 7 8 9 10 09 08 07

TABLE OF CONTENTS

Words that appear in the glossary are printed in
boldface type the first time they occur in the text.

Chapter 1:

Where Should We Have the Party?

School is almost over. The children in the neighborhood are planning a summer block party. Everyone who lives in the apartments will be invited. They will meet at Emma's apartment. Her grandmother will help plan the party.

The neighborhood children plan the summer block party.

First, they will choose where to have the party. The children have three ideas. They can have the party at one of their apartments. The courtyard between the apartment buildings is another choice. They can also have the party at the neighborhood park.

Clancy lists the three choices. The children need to pick one place for the party. They will vote to decide. The children write their names on a sheet of paper. They vote for the best place to have the block party.

Where Should We Have the Block Party?

Apartment	Courtyard	Park
	Ruben	Sam
	Gloria	
	Mai	

The **results** are in. Most of the children think the courtyard will be a good place for the block party. There will be lots of room to play in the area between the apartment buildings. The party will be close to all the neighbors, too.

Where Should We Have the Block Party?

Apartment	Courtyard	Park
Clancy	Ruben	Sam
	Gloria	Kim
	Mai	Emma
	Jesse	
	Sophie	

Chapter 2:
What Should We Do at the Party?

Next, they will decide what kind of food to have at the party.

Should they have popcorn? What about pretzels or carrots with dip?

Sophie thinks string cheese and sliced apples are good choices.

Jesse writes the ideas on his paper. Everyone votes for a favorite food. Jesse makes **tally** marks on his tally table to record the votes.

What would the neighbors like to eat? They will ask some of the neighbors. Then they will add this **data** to the tally table.

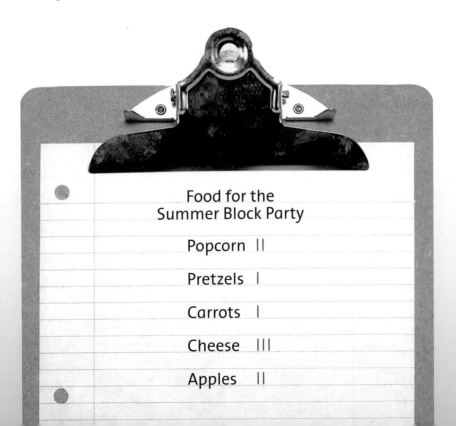

Food for the
Summer Block Party

Popcorn ||

Pretzels |

Carrots |

Cheese |||

Apples ||

Lemonade, water, milk, and juice could be served at the party.

Emma's grandmother says they should have drinks at the party. Ruben thinks lemonade would be great. They can have water to drink, too. Some people might want milk or orange juice.

Gloria lists the choices. The children vote for their favorite drinks.

Gloria draws a dot for each vote. Lemonade has the most votes. Will the neighbors like lemonade, too? She will ask them to find out.

Drinks for the Summer Block Party

Musical chairs would be a fun game to play at the party.

They should play a game at the party. It would be fun to have a game everyone can play. Musical chairs is fun to play. Some people would like freeze tag. Everyone could join in a treasure hunt.

Ruben makes a list of game choices. The children vote for their favorite games. Ruben records this data on his grid paper. He makes a **bar graph.**

The children vote to play musical chairs at the block party.

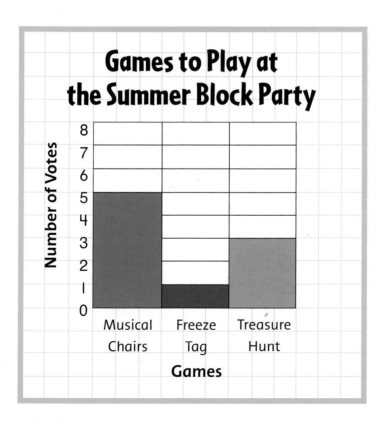

Chapter 3:
Which One Is Your Favorite?

The children have chosen their favorite food, drink, and game. Now they will talk to some neighbors. The children will ask them to vote, too.

The children ask the neighbors to vote for their favorite food, drink, and game.

The children will meet at Emma's apartment again. They will add the data to their graphs. Then they will finish their plans for the party.

Mrs. Hernandez votes for musical chairs.

Mrs. Hernandez is Jesse's mom. She thinks musical chairs would be the most fun for everyone. Ruben records her vote on his graph. Now there are six votes for musical chairs.

Mr. Orta votes for sliced apples.

Mr. Orta lives next door to Sophie. He thinks sliced apples would be a good snack for the party. Jesse makes a tally mark next to "sliced apples" on his tally table. Mrs. Orta votes for sliced apples, too. Now there are four votes for apples.

Chapter 4:
The Results Are In!

The children talk with many neighbors.
Then they return to Emma's apartment.
They look at the data.

Gloria shows the graph of drink choices. Lemonade has the most votes. Eight people said lemonade is their favorite drink. They will have lemonade at the block party.

Drinks for the Summer Block Party

Jesse shares the tally table he made. Two foods have the same number of votes. String cheese and sliced apples each have five votes. The children will serve both foods at the block party.

Food for the
Summer Block Party

Popcorn |||

Pretzels |

Carrots ||

Cheese |||||

Apples |||||

Ruben shows the bar graph he made. The longest bar on the graph is for musical chairs. It got the most votes. The children think everyone will like that game.

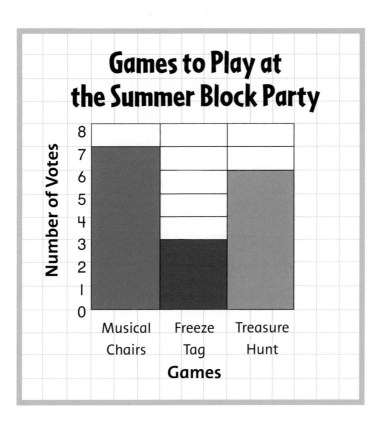

The plans for the summer block party are complete.

The plans for the party are done. The children will serve string cheese and sliced apples. They will have lemonade to drink. They will ask everyone to play musical chairs.

Now the children can invite the neighbors to the summer block party. Everyone will have fun!

Come to the
Summer Block Party
in the Courtyard
Next Saturday!

Glossary

bar graph: a drawing that uses bars of different lengths to show different numbers or amounts

data: facts or information

results: outcomes

tally: the mark in a tally table that stands for one thing

About the Author

Jennifer Marrewa is a former elementary school teacher who writes children's books, poetry, nonfiction, and supplemental learning materials. She lives in California with her husband and two young children.